TWELVE DAYS OF CHRISTMAS WITH ROALD DAHL

FESTIVE THINGS TO MAKE AND DO

PUFFIN

Contents

On the first day of Christmas my true love gave to me . . .

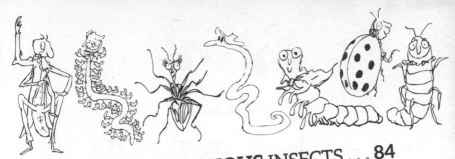

WELCOME

to Roald Dahl's

festive feast of SPROUTS

and SNOZZCUMBERS!

It's time to celebrate Christmas with some of Roald Dahl's best-loved characters. Try out lots of seasonal recipes, including **Chocolate and Brussels Sprout Pie** and the BFG's **Festive Frobscottle**, read the Twits' guide to being **naughty** at Christmas's (guaranteed to put you at the top of Father Christmas's Naughty List), and even make your very own **Gingerbread Chocolate Factory!**

What better way to **start celebrating Christmas** than with this original Christmas poem by Roald Dahl and drawing by Quentin Blake? Dahl wrote it for Great Ormond Street Hospital for a fundraising Christmas card.

Where art thou, Mother Christmas?

Where art thou, Mother Christmas?
I only wish I knew
Why Father should get all the praise
And no one mentions you.

I'll bet you buy the presents
And wrap them large and small
While all the time that rotten swine
Pretends he's done it all.

So Hail To Mother Christmas
Who shoulders all the work!
And down with Father Christmas,
That unmitigated jerk!

On the

FIRST

day of
Christmas

**my true love
gave to me . . .**

ONE
MATILDA
IN THE
LIBRARY

Matilda's
Clever Christmas Spinners

It's no secret that Matilda is a **whizz** with words!
Trace these festive word spinners and arrows on to card, then push paper fasteners through the middle of each pair. Spin the arrows in number order to create your own clever Christmas combinations!

For example:

'Merry **elves** pirouette stupidly around the **NORTH POLE**.'

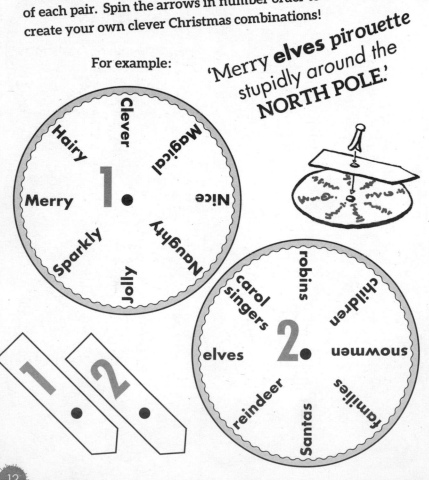

Spinner 1: Clever, Magical, Nice, Naughty, Jolly, Sparkly, Merry, Hairy — **1.**

Spinner 2: robins, children, snowmen, families, Santas, reindeer, elves, carol singers — **2.**

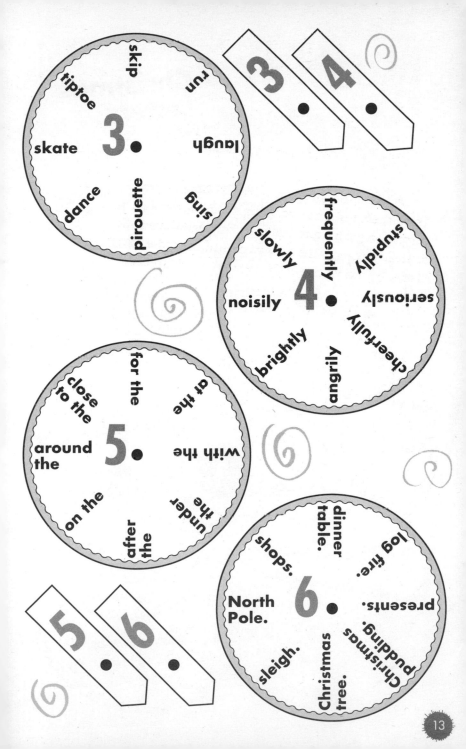

Spinner 3: skip, run, laugh, sing, pirouette, dance, skate, tiptoe

Spinner 4: frequently, stupidly, seriously, angrily, cheerfully, brightly, noisily, slowly

Spinner 5: for the, at the, with the, under the, after the, on the, around the, close to the

Spinner 6: dinner table, log fire, presents, Christmas pudding, Christmas tree, sleigh, North Pole, shops

Invisible Christmas Letters

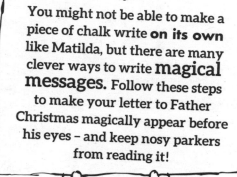

You might not be able to make a piece of chalk write **on its own** like Matilda, but there are many clever ways to write **magical messages**. Follow these steps to make your letter to Father Christmas magically appear before his eyes – and keep nosy parkers from reading it!

You will need

❄ A bowl
❄ Half a lemon
❄ A spoon
❄ Water
❄ A cotton bud, feather quill pen or toothpick to write with
❄ Sheets of white paper
❄ A heat source like sunlight or a light bulb

What to do

1

Squeeze some lemon juice into a bowl and **stir** in a few drops of water with a spoon.

2

Dip your quill pen, toothpick or cotton bud into the juice and **write** your letter to Father Christmas on a piece of paper.

3

Send your message to Father Christmas. He'll **know** what to do but, just in case, you could **add a note** asking him to hold it in the sunlight or close to a light bulb.

Keep it simple

If all you have is paper and pencils, you can **still** write an invisible letter! Simply take **two pieces of paper** and lay one over the other. Write your message on the top piece, pressing down **very hard**. Remove this top sheet and destroy it, then **post** the bottom sheet to Father Christmas, asking him to shade over your letter with a soft pencil to make the message **magically appear!**

No lemon to hand?

If you have a **white wax crayon**, you can use it to write your letter to Father Christmas on white paper so that it's **invisible**. Just ask him to brush over the paper with **watercolour paint** to reveal what it says!

Matilda's Word-a-Day
Christmas Countdown

Be an **extraordinary** genius just like Matilda and impress your friends by learning a **NEW WORD** every day of December until Christmas!

1 **Anticipating** – expecting. *'The children were eagerly anticipating Christmas.'*

2 **Borborygmus** – gurgling or rumbling noise made by fluid and gas passing through the intenstines. *'If you eat an excessive amount of Brussels sprouts you might hear borborygmus!'*

3 **Cacophony** – a harsh, jarring combination of sounds. *'The school's Christmas production ended in a cacophony of deafening Christmas bells!'*

4 **Diddly-squat** – anything (or nothing!). *'Miss Trunchbull probably doesn't give diddly-squat about Christmas.'*

5 **Discombobulated** – confused. *'Mr Wormwood was discombobulated by Matilda's prank.'*

6 **Effervescence** – the fizz or bubbles in a liquid. *'Make the BFG's festive frobscottle on pages 54–55 to experience effervescence.'*

7 **Ephemeral** – lasting for a very short amount of time. 'The excitement of Christmas can be quite ephemeral.'

8 **Fandangle** – something that's decorative with little use. 'Grandma didn't understand what all the fandangles on her Christmas present were.'

9 **Fussbudget** – someone who is fussy. 'Miss Trunchbull has no patience with children who are fussbudgets.'

10 **Outlandish** – looking or sounding strange or out of the ordinary. 'Mr Wormwood wears outlandish suits to work.'

11 **Guttersnipe** – a naughty, scruffy child who spends a lot of their time outside, usually on the street. 'Matilda wouldn't have been surprised if Miss Trunchbull had called her a little guttersnipe!'

12 **Harrumph** – to clear the throat loudly. 'The old man harrumphed before he sang each Christmas carol.'

13 **Hubbub** – a chaotic racket created by a group of people. 'All the hubbub of Christmas can be too much for some people.'

14 **Humdinger** – a brilliant or extraordinary person or thing. 'It was a humdinger of a funny story.'

15 **Infinitesimal** – exceptionally small. 'Mr Wormwood's brain is infinitesimal.'

16 **Jabberwocky** – made-up language or nonsense. 'Roald Dahl made up his own brilliant jabberwocky, otherwise known as "gobblefunk".'

17 Lollapalooza – someone or something that's really impressive. *'It's a lollapalooza, just like Roald Dahl's other books.'*

18 Malapropism – a word that's used incorrectly to mean a similar-sounding one, for example: 'he was putrified' instead of 'he was petrified'. *'Mrs Wormwood is the kind of lady who would probably fall victim to malapropisms without realizing.'*

19 Miasma – a distasteful or disagreeable smell. *'With his disgusting beard, it comes as no surprise that Mr Twit has a miasma of stale food about him.'*

20 Paraphernalia – random items, specifically things needed for a certain activity. *'Mr Wormwood has all the paraphernalia for making dodgy cars to sell to people.'*

21 Resplendent – beautiful and remarkable through being gloriously bright. *'The Christmas tree was shiny from top to toe, resplendent with tinsel and fairy lights.'*

22 Splendiferous – splendid. *'What a splendiferous Christmas dinner!'*

23 Tintinnabulation – a bell-like sound. *'The tiny tintinnabulation of Christmas bells could be heard.'*

24 Wunderkind – someone who achieves great success while still young. *'Matilda is a wunderkind!'*

25 Yuletide – an old word for Christmas. *'The children's minds were full of Yuletide wonder.'*

December

by Roald Dahl, from *My Year*

This, as you all know, is the month when two good things happen. The term ends and Christmas comes. For many of you, the whole of December is spent counting the days to Christmas and you can see a stirring among the parents as they begin to perform all the usual rituals like making lists of presents and sending out cards and finally buying the tree itself. By now you will have told them what you are wishing for. I approve very much of children who make their own Christmas cards, and whenever I get one of those I am deeply touched because I know the time and effort that has gone into making it. The cards I hate getting are the ones that have on them a colour photograph of the senders standing proudly somewhere or other surrounded by their offspring. You can be half blinded by the self-satisfaction shining out of their faces as they stare back at you from the card.

Even if you live in a town you can notice several rather unusual birds in your gardens at this time of year. We have a cotoneaster shrub on the wall of our house which is always covered with brilliant red berries in December, and this is a special favourite of a lovely bird called the waxwing. You may swear you have never seen a waxwing and have never even heard the name, but the odds are you *have* seen one several times and simply haven't taken note of it. Waxwings come into Britain in December to escape the freezing weather in Norway and Sweden, but they don't come regularly. Some years they arrive in swarms, other years they don't come at all. If you look in your Bird Book you will see that the waxwing has a marvellous pale brown parrotlike crest on its head. The wings are striped black and white with a flash of scarlet on them, and the tail has a vivid yellow bar at the end of it. The trouble is they are so striking to look at that idiots shoot them for their feathers.

In December the tawny owls in our orchard start hooting like mad all through the night. You will quite often also hear them if you live in a town where they exist by pouncing on starlings and sparrows while they are roosting and fast asleep.

As I write, I am remembering something I did during the Christmas holidays when I was either nine or ten, I can't be sure which. We lived in Kent then, in a fairly large house that had a wide lane and a public footpath running through our land at the back of the house. For Christmas that year I had been given a fine Meccano set as my main present, and I lay in bed that night after the celebrations were over thinking that I must build something with my new Meccano that had never been built before. In the end I decided I would make a device that was capable of 'bombing' from the air the pedestrians using the public footpath across our land.

Briefly my plan was as follows: I would stretch a wire all the way from the high roof of our house to the old garage on the other side of the footpath. Then I would construct from my Meccano a machine that would hang from the wire by a grooved wheel (there was such a wheel in my Meccano box) and this machine would hopefully run down the wire at great speed dropping its bombs on the unwary walkers underneath.

Next morning, filled with the enthusiasm that grips all great inventors, I climbed on to the roof of our house by the skylight and wrapped one end of the long roll of wire around a chimney. I threw the rest of the wire into the garden below and went back down myself through the skylight. I carried the wire across the garden, over the fence, across the footpath, over the next fence and into our land on the other side. I now pulled the wire very tight and fixed it with a big nail to the top of the door of the old garage. The total length of the wire was about one hundred yards. So far so good.

Next I set about constructing from the Meccano my bombing machine, or chariot as I called it. I put the wheel at the top, and then running down from the wheel I made a strong column about two feet long. At the lower end of this column, I fixed two arms that projected outwards at right angles, one on either side, and along these arms I suspended five empty Heinz soup tins. The whole thing looked something like this:

I carried it up to the roof and hung it on the wire. Then I attached one end of a ball of string to the lower end of the chariot and let it rip, playing out the string as it went. It was wonderful. Because the wire sloped steeply from the roof of the house all the way to the other end, the chariot careered down the wire at terrific speed, across the garden and over the footpath, and it didn't stop until it hit the old garage door on the far side. Great. I was ready to go.

With the string, I hauled the chariot back to the roof. And now, from a jug I filled all the five soup tins with water. I lay flat on the roof waiting for a victim. I knew I wouldn't have to wait long because the footpath was much used by people taking their dogs for walks in the wood beyond.

Soon two ladies dressed in tweed skirts and jackets and each wearing a hat, came strolling up the path with a revolting little Pekinese dog on a lead. I knew I had to time this carefully, so when they were very nearly but not quite directly under the wire, I let my chariot go. Down she went, making a wonderful screeching-humming noise as the metal wheel ran down the wire and the string ran through my fingers at great speed. Bombing from a height is never easy. I had to guess when my chariot was directly over the target, and when that moment came, I jerked the string. The chariot stopped dead and the tins swung upside down and all the water tipped out. The ladies, who had halted and looked up on hearing the rushing noise of my chariot overhead, caught the cascade of water full in their faces. It was tremendous. A bull's-eye first time. The women screamed. I lay flat on the roof so as not to be seen, peering over the edge, and I saw the women shouting and waving their arms. Then they came marching straight into our garden through the gate at the back and crossed the garden and hammered on the door. I nipped down smartly through the skylight and did a bunk.

Later on, at lunch, my mother fixed me with a steely eye and told me she was confiscating my Meccano set for the rest of the holidays. But for days afterwards I experienced the pleasant warm glow that comes to all of us when we have brought off a major triumph.

I hope you all have a lovely Christmas and a super holiday.

On the

SECOND

day of
Christmas

my true love
gave to me . . .

TWO
SMELLY
TWITS

The Naughty List

This lot are **definitely** on Father Christmas's Naughty List! Check out their stats, then fill in the number you think they are on the list – **number 1** being the naughtiest.

Mr and Mrs Twit

- Position on Naughty List: . . . .
- Naughtiness: **10/10**
- Smelliness: **9/10**

Miss Trunchbull

- Position on Naughty List: . . . .
- Naughtiness: **9/10**
- Brute strength: **10/10**

The Bloodbottler

- Position on Naughty List: . . . .
- Naughtiness: **7/10**
- Giganticness: **10/10**

Aunt Spiker and Aunt Sponge

- Position on Naughty List: ....
- Naughtiness: **9/10**
- Oppositeness: **10/10**

The Grand High Witch

- Position on Naughty List: ....
- Naughtiness: **9/10**
- Hatred of children: **10/10**

Boggis, Bunce and Bean

- Position on Naughty List: ....
- Naughtiness: **7/10**
- Cruelty to animals: **8/10**

The Enormous Crocodile

- Position on Naughty List: ....
- Naughtiness: **8/10**
- Sharpness of teeth: **10/10**

A Recipe for *Chocolate* and Brussels Sprout Pie

It's a well-known fact that grown-ups **adore** eating vegetables nearly as much as they adore making younger people eat vegetables. So they are bound to **LOVE** this delightful pie. Why not rustle one up at the weekend, feed it to the grown-ups of your choice and **THEN** get them to guess **what's in it?**

PS If they make lots of weird noises like '**BLEURGH**' and '**EEUCH**', tell them that it's good for them and not to whinge. Just like they tell you!

You will need

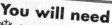

- ❄ 1 spoonful of butter or margarine or posh spread made from olives
- ❄ A pie dish
- ❄ A rolling pin
- ❄ 1 packet of puff pastry
- ❄ 1 bag of Brussels sprouts
- ❄ 1 bar of very dark chocolate
- ❄ 1 egg
- ❄ An oven
- ❄ 1 group of grown-ups, preferably the healthy sort

OPTIONAL INGREDIENTS: cabbage, Marmite, chocolate sprinkles, syrup, baked beans, mashed pumpkin, jam, tinned carrots and sardines. **Mmm.**

What to do

1 **Rub** the butter, margarine or posh spread made from olives around your pie dish.

2 **Roll out** two circles of pastry. Put one of them into your pie dish.

3 Put the **Brussels sprouts** into the pie dish.

4 Break the **chocolate** up into squares and put that in too.

5 **Add** as many of the optional ingredients as you like.

6 **Place** the other circle of pastry on top of the pie dish and **seal the pastry** round the edges by pinching them together.

7 **Paint** the top of the pie with **beaten egg**, just to make it look super appetizing when it's cooked.

8 **Ask a grown-up** to help you pop it in the oven. Bake for 45 minutes to an hour at 190° Celsius.

Try to find out whether the grown-ups like Brussels sprouts and chocolate first!

Vile Twitsmas

Cracker Jokes

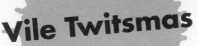

Turn **Christmas** into a riot of repulsive mirth with these **side-splitting** Twitsmas cracker **jokes!**

Mr Twit: Get me a dog for Christmas!
Mrs Twit: No, you'll have turkey like everyone else!

What do you call a greedy elf?
Elfish!

What's the best thing to put into your Christmas dinner?
Your teeth!

What do you get if you eat Christmas decorations?
Tinselitus!

The Twits' Guide to Being ~~Nice~~ NAUGHTY at Christmas

Follow the Twits' **really clever** and **very nasty** Christmas tricks, and you'll soon be at the top of Father Christmas's **Naughty List!**

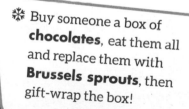

❄ Buy someone a box of **chocolates**, eat them all and replace them with **Brussels sprouts**, then gift-wrap the box!

❄ Offer to make **drinks** for everyone at dinner, but make them undrinkable by using **jelly**.

❄ Offer to take a family **Christmas picture** and replace everyone's eyes with stick-on **googly eyes**.

❄ Make a beautiful-looking Christmas **dessert**: dust a real wooden log with icing sugar and decorate it with holly, then serve it as a **Yule log!**

Mischievous Merriment

Play these **alternative** Christmas games with your family and friends at Christmastime, and fill the house with much **MISCHIEVOUS** merriment!

You will need
- ❄ Sticky notes
- ❄ Pens
- ❄ A vile imagination

What am I?
(the revolting substances version)

How to play

1 Write different **revolting** substances down on a number of sticky notes. (Things like 'reindeer poo', 'elf's earwax', 'Santa's toe fluff' and 'glow-in-the-dark snot' work **particularly well**.)

2 Get a group of people together to play. **Each person** in turn has a sticky note placed on their **forehead** which only the other players can see.

3 The person with the **sticky note** on their forehead asks the other players 'yes' or 'no' **questions** about the substance on their head in order to figure out what it is. For example: '**Am I green?**'

4 The **winner** is the person who figures out which **revolting** substance they are in the **fewest** questions.

Nasty present list

How to play

1 In a **group**, start by saying 'For Christmas, I want . . .' and add something beginning with **A** (for example: 'an adder'). Make sure it's disgusting, or a thing that someone might not want as a **present**!

2 The next person says the **first** thing on the list ('an adder') and then something beginning with **B** (for example: 'a bogey').

3 Continue round the group, working through the **alphabet**, adding one more horrid item to the end each time. Start again when someone forgets items in the list.

Guess
the gross gift

How to play

You will need
❅ An old Christmas stocking or one that is washable
❆ Some gross gifts to fill your stocking with.
For example: slime, cold spaghetti, baked beans (out of the can), an old sponge, a rubber spider, fake poo, etc.

1 Fill the stocking with a number of different **gross gifts**.

2 Ask your family and friends to take it in turns to put their **hand** in the stocking without looking inside and **guess** what the gifts are.

3 The person who correctly identifies the most gross gifts is the **winner** – perhaps they could **keep** all the gross gifts as a prize!

Wormy Spaghetti

Fed up with eating **turkey** during Christmastime? This is what Mrs Twit makes for Mr Twit when he's not eating **bird pie**!

Serves 4–5

No worms are harmed in the making of this recipe!

You'll need a grown-up to help you!

You will need

- ❄ 2 large saucepans
- ❄ food processor

Sauce:
- ❄ 2 tbsp sunflower oil
- ❄ 1 onion, chopped
- ❄ 1 clove of garlic, crushed
- ❄ 400g tin of plum tomatoes
- ❄ 1 tbsp tomato purée

- ❄ 1 tbsp parsley, chopped
- ❄ 1 bay leaf
- ❄ 1 tsp sugar
- ❄ 2 carrots, grated
- ❄ salt and pepper

- ❄ 2 tsp olive oil
- ❄ 275g spaghetti
- ❄ 170g Cheddar cheese (grated)

What to do

1 **With a grown-up's help**, heat the sunflower oil in a saucepan and sweat the onion and garlic until soft.

2 Add the remaining ingredients for the sauce **except** the carrot, bring to the boil and allow to **simmer** for thirty minutes.

3 Remove the bay leaf and **liquidize** the sauce until smooth.

4 Return the sauce to the saucepan, **taste** for seasoning and keep warm.

5 Meanwhile bring a large saucepan of water to the **boil**. Break the spaghetti into thirds, and add it to the boiling water with the olive oil and salt. Cook until **tender**, and then **drain**.

6 **Reheat** the sauce and mix in the carrot until it is warm.

7 Share out the **spaghetti** on each serving plate, **spoon** over the sauce and **garnish** with the grated cheese.

Serve with a tasty green salad!

35

On the

THIRD

day of Christmas

my true love gave to me . . .

THREE
NAUGHTY
MUGGLE-
WUMPS

Nutty Christmas FORTUNE Decorations

The monkey in *The Giraffe and the Pelly and Me* liked walnuts so much he dreamed about them! 'A walnut fresh from the tree is scrumptious-galumptious...'

Follow these steps to make some nutty Christmas fortune decorations for your Christmas tree.

You will need

❄ Walnuts (and a grown-up to help you crack the shells in half)
❄ Paper
❄ Pens
❄ Glue
❄ Gold paint or glitter
❄ A paintbrush
❄ Ribbon
❄ Pins

What to do

1

Ask a grown-up to help you **crack** each of the walnuts so that you have **two half-shells**, and remove the insides.

2

Write a **secret** Christmas fortune on a small piece of paper to put inside each of the shells. For example: 'You will get your Christmas dinner stuck in your beard.'

3

When the paper is inside, **glue** the two halves of each walnut shell back together.

4

Paint the outside of the shells with gold paint or glitter. Once the paint is dry, ask a grown-up to help you **pin a ribbon** to the top of each shell in order to hang it on the tree.

5 On **Christmas morning**, hand out the decorations so that each person can open their walnut shell and read their message.

Note
Remember to tell everyone that the nuts are not edible, and don't give them to anyone who is allergic to nuts.

THE GRUBBER'S
Christmas Specials

Christmas wouldn't be Christmas without sweets from The Grubber, the **wonderful** sweet shop! Read about its bestselling treats below, and then invent some **special** festive candies ...

 Scarlet Scorchdroppers – guaranteed to make you as **warm as toast** even if you're standing stark naked at the North Pole in midwinter.

 Giant Wangdoodles – have huge ripe red strawberries hidden inside their crispy chocolate crusts!

Electric Fizzcocklers – make every hair stand **straight up on end** as soon as you pop one into your mouth!

Pishlets – help you whistle.

Stickjaw – for talkative parents.

Mint Jujubes – will give you **green** teeth for a month!

Devil's Drenchers – after sucking one of these for a minute, you can set your breath alight and blow a huge **column of fire** into the air!

Willy Wonka Rainbow Drops – suck them and you can **spit** in seven different colours!

Write your own special **Christmas** sweet inventions here:

. . . .

. . . .

. . . .

. . . .

. . . .

Almost BOTTOMLESS Gift List

The Duke and Duchess of Hampshire in *The Giraffe and the Pelly and Me* had **bucketloads** of money and jewels! If you were the richest boy or girl on earth, what PRESENTS would you buy? Create an almost bottomless **Christmas gift list** here!

For my friends

....
....
....
....
....
....
....
....
....
....
....
....

For myself

....
....
....
....
....
....
....
....
....
....
....
....
....

On the

FOURTH

day of Christmas

my true love gave to me . . .

FOUR
REPULSANT
SNOZZCUMBERS

Christmas Eve Dreams

The BFG told Sophie that *'Dreams is very mystical things!'* Use these **dream jars** to create the most magical and mystical wondercrump dream for the night before Christmas! Make sure it's a phizzwizard – they're the best!

Snowy backdrop

Friends

A TOUCH OF MAGIC

Starry sky

Flying

FAMILY

Sparkling icicles

Gifts

Presents

A SPRINKLING OF GLITTER

A log fire

Christmas **hugs**

Delicious food

Lots of **wonderful** surprises!

46

Dream Jar
Snow Globe

Follow the steps to make your own *magical* Christmas **dream jar!**

You will need
 A watertight glass jar
 Modelling clay
 Christmas cake decorations (small enough to fit inside the jar)
 Water
 Glitter

What to do

1

Take the **lid** off your jar and cover the inside of the lid with **modelling clay**.

2

Position your **Christmas decorations** in the clay to make a Christmas scene. **Push them in firmly** and make sure they won't come out.

3

Fill the jar with water and some **glitter**. Screw the lid of your jar back on **tightly**.

4

Shake your jar and watch your Christmassy dream come to life!

Stick the Ears on the BFG

Play this fun *BFG* game at a **Christmas party!**

You will need

* A large piece of paper
* Pens
* A piece of card
* Scissors
* Sticky tack
* Something to use as a blindfold

What to do

1 Find a **large** piece of paper and **copy** this picture of the BFG on to it. Draw the picture as big as you can to fill the paper!

2 Copy the BFG's ears (see page 52) on to the piece of card and cut out. Put some sticky tack on the back of each ear.

3 Find an old tie or tea towel to use as a **blindfold**.

4 Take it in turns to put on the blindfold and **stick** the ears on the BFG, making a note of where each person put them.

5 The person who gets **both** of the BFG's ears closest to where they should be is the **winner!**

50

51

Sophie's *Christmas* NIGHTIE

Colour in SOPHIE'S special Christmas nightdress to wear on **Christmas Eve.**

Festive Frobscottle

Make the BFG and your friends and family a **delumptious** drink this Christmas – festive frobscottle!

'IT'S GLUMMY!'

You will need
- ❄ Lemonade
- ❄ Lime cordial or green food colouring
- ❄ Raspberry syrup
- ❄ A measuring jug
- ❄ Drinking glasses
- ❄ A jar of popping candy
- ❄ A spoon
- ❄ Paper straws

What to do

1 Depending on **how many** glasses of festive frobscottle you want to make, pour the lemonade and enough lime cordial or green food colouring to make it **look green** into a measuring jug.

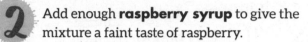

2 Add enough **raspberry syrup** to give the mixture a faint taste of raspberry.

3 Find some drinking glasses and put a spoonful of **popping candy** in the bottom of each glass.

4 **Pour** the liquid over the popping candy and watch the green stuff **fizz** and **bubble!**

5 **Serve** each glass with a paper straw and enjoy the **wonderful** bubbly stuff!

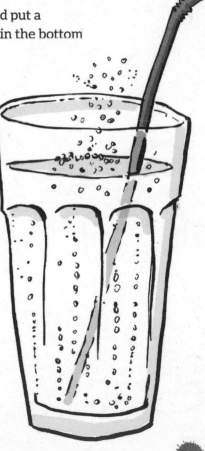

Seasonal
SNOZZCUMBER
Recipes

How many **different** festive dishes can you make out of **snozzcumbers** for the BFG's Christmas feast?

For example, you could have **snozzcumber canapés**, followed by **roast snozzcumber**, and **snozzcumber trifle** with lashings of **snozzcumber custard** for pudding, with **festive frobscottle** to wash it all down!

Menu

GIANT
Feast Time!

Draw the BFG's **GIANT**
Christmas snozzcumber
feast on the table for him.

GIANT
Pop-Up Christmas Card

Make a pop-up Big Friendly Giant card for your friends or family this Christmas.

You will need

❄ 2 large pieces of white card (A3 or larger)
❄ Pencils and pens for drawing
❄ A ruler
❄ Scissors
❄ A glue stick
❄ Shiny paper to decorate

What to do

1 Fold one large white piece of card in half (**widthways**). Fold and cut the other piece of card **lengthways**, then divide it into four sections by drawing four faint lines with a pencil and a ruler, as shown. Sections 2 and 4 must be the **same size**, but sections 1 and 4 can be whatever size suits your drawing. Write the numbers in pencil on the back of the card.

2 **Draw** the BFG down the centre of the narrow card, dividing him into three sections as shown. Try to put his head and body in section 1 and his legs over sections 2 and 3. (Leave section 4 blank.) **Cut out** your drawing of the BFG and fold along the lines of each section, as shown below.

3 Glue the blank **section 4** to one side of the fold line inside the first folded card from step 1. The end of the tab must line up with the **fold** in the centre.

4 Glue the back of section 1 to the other side of the folded card, as shown, then close the card, **press down** firmly and wait for the glue to dry.

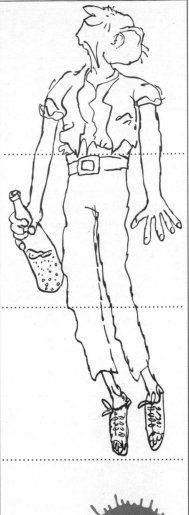

Here it's the BFG, but you can draw anyone!

5 Open out the card carefully and the BFG should pop up! **Decorate** the front of your card with glitter and other Christmassy things, then write your message inside.

59

On the

FIFTH

day of
Christmas

**my true love
gave to me . . .**

FIVE
GOLDEN
TICKETS

Christmas Calendar

You will need

- ❄ 25 gold-coloured envelopes (big enough to hold one chocolate treat each)
- ❄ Pens
- ❄ 25 mouth-wateringly delicious chocolate treats
- ❄ Clothes pegs
- ❄ String or ribbon
- ❄ Candy canes for decoration

'Mr Willy Wonka is the most amazing, the most fantastic, the most extraordinary chocolate maker the world has ever seen!'

Make a chocolate Christmas countdown calendar that the marvellous magician with chocolate – Mr Wonka – would definitely approve of!

What to do

1

Write the numbers 1–25 on the golden envelopes, then put a **delicious** chocolate inside each one.

2

Attach each envelope to your **ribbon** or string with a peg. **Make sure** the opening is at the pegged end so the chocolates don't fall out! **Ask a grown-up** to help you hang up the ribbon of golden envelopes.

3

Make your calendar **even more** festive and sweet by hanging **candy canes** over the top of the ribbon or string, as shown.

4

Open one envelope **each day** in December in the run-up to Christmas, and enjoy a **special treat!**

What ROALD DAHL thought about *Christmas*

Roald Dahl **loved** giving presents, but he **hated** Christmas.
Here's what he thought about it:

1. Christmas is for children.

2. Grown-ups should try to make Christmas fun for children.

3. Christmas is a bonanza for shopkeepers. Everyone else gets poor.

4 Home-made Christmas cards are the best things ever.

5 Christmas cards with photos of the senders on the front are the worst things ever.

6 Presents should be given to family members and no one else.

7 Goose tastes wonderful . . .

8 . . . but turkey is one of the most tasteless meats that it is possible to find.

9 The best presents of all are the simplest ones . . .

10 . . . like a glass jar of wine gums.

Christmas Presents

❄ Use paper straws with chocolate bars taped to the top to create a festive chocolate Christmas bouquet! Then wrap the bottom with green or red tissue paper.

❄ Add pipe-cleaner antlers, googly eyes and pom-poms to tubes of chocolates and sweets.

❄ Fill recycled glass jars with hot chocolate and marshmallows for the perfect Christmas Eve hot cocoa gift.

❄ Make Father Christmas **sleighs** out of candy canes, chocolate bars and mini chocolate Santas.

❄ Make a chocolate-bar **Christmas tree** where each of the branches is a chocolate bar, and plant it in a **pot of sweets!**

❄ Fill clean recycled **glass jars** with your friends' favourite sweets, then decorate them with ribbons, glitter glue and Christmas shapes to make them look fun and festive.

❄ Make marshmallow **snow people** on lollipop sticks, with sweet laces for scarves, mini sweets stuck on with icing to make buttons, eyes and a nose, and a **chocolate cup** as a hat.

Strawberry-flavoured CHOCOLATE-COATED

fudge

You will need

- ❄ 20x25cm shallow baking tin
- ❄ Greaseproof paper
- ❄ A large saucepan
- ❄ A sugar thermometer
- ❄ A palette knife
- ❄ Shaped cutters
- ❄ 450g caster sugar
- ❄ 100g unsalted butter
- ❄ 175ml evaporated milk
- ❄ A few generous drops of pink food colouring
- ❄ A generous ½ teaspoon strawberry food flavouring
- ❄ 100g melted chocolate for dipping

Makes enough for ten GREEDY children!

Ask a grown-up to heat and beat the sugar as it's very tricky!

What to do

1 **Line the tin** with buttered greaseproof paper.

2 Put all the ingredients **except** flavouring and colouring into a large **heavy-bottomed** saucepan and place over a low heat.

3 Stir **occasionally**. Once the sugar has dissolved, gently boil the mixture with a grown-up's help. **Stir all the time** (to prevent sticking and burning on the bottom of the pan). Place the sugar thermometer into the saucepan and boil to **soft ball** (118°C). This takes about 5 minutes.

4 Take the pan off the heat, stir until the **bubbles** subside and then add the **flavouring** and the **colouring**.

5 **Mix rapidly** with a wooden spoon until the mixture thickens and becomes **granular**, approx. 3 minutes.

6 Pour the fudge into the lined tin and leave to **set**. If necessary, **smooth** with a palette knife dipped in boiling water.

7 With shaped cutters, **cut** the fudge and **dip** one side into the melted chocolate; or **decorate** with piped chocolate, creating different patterns.

A super Christmas present!

Gingerbread Chocolate Factory

You will need
* ❄ Gingerbread-house kit
* ❄ Icing
* ❄ Liquorice sticks – black and strawberry
* ❄ Long marshmallows
* ❄ Lollipop sticks or straws
* ❄ Chocolate buttons
* ❄ Brightly coloured jelly sweets
* ❄ Candy canes
* ❄ Swirly lollipops
* ❄ Pretzels
* ❄ Icing pens
* ❄ Edible gold glitter
* ❄ Chocolate sticks
* ❄ Rainbow sprinkles
* ❄ Triangle-shaped chocolate bar

Transform a gingerbread house into Mr Willy Wonka's incredible chocolate factory with these **amazing** decorating ideas!

What to do

Follow the **instructions** for making your gingerbread house **then**, when you get to the decorating stage, use these tips to help **transform** it into a gingerbread chocolate factory!

Use candy canes and swirly lollipops to make trees around the factory.

Use edible gold glitter to make your gingerbread chocolate factory nice and shiny.

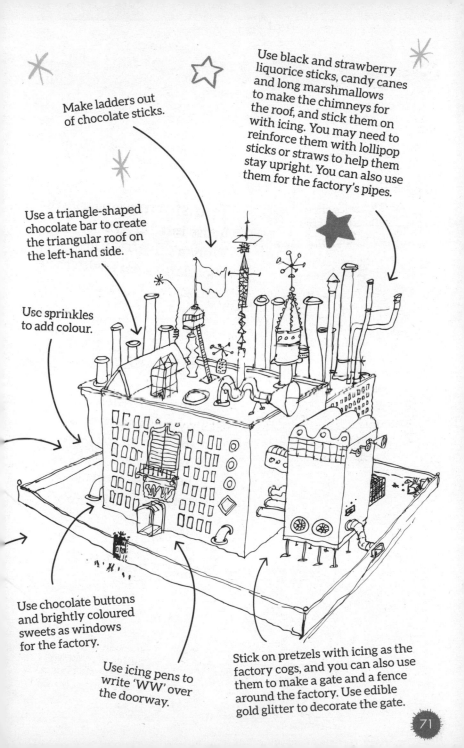

Make ladders out of chocolate sticks.

Use black and strawberry liquorice sticks, candy canes and long marshmallows to make the chimneys for the roof, and stick them on with icing. You may need to reinforce them with lollipop sticks or straws to help them stay upright. You can also use them for the factory's pipes.

Use a triangle-shaped chocolate bar to create the triangular roof on the left-hand side.

Use sprinkles to add colour.

Use chocolate buttons and brightly coloured sweets as windows for the factory.

Use icing pens to write 'WW' over the doorway.

Stick on pretzels with icing as the factory cogs, and you can also use them to make a gate and a fence around the factory. Use edible gold glitter to decorate the gate.

71

On the

SIXTH

day of
Christmas

**my true love
gave to me . . .**

SIX
CUNNING
FOXES

A letter from young Roald Dahl
(from *Boy*)

Dec. 12th 1926

St. Peter's
Weston-super-Mare

Dear Mama,

This is my last letter to you this term. We had a special treat last night, we all hung up our stockings, and when it was dark Matron came in dressed up as Father Xmas, and put things in our stockings, I got a kind of a musical box and a soldier on a horse in mine. The same night she hung up hers outside her door and we all put things in it. It was full in the end. We start exams next Tuesday and they go on till Thursday.

I AM COMING HOME NEXT FRIDAY

Fantastic Fox Stocking

You will need

❄ 3 thin sheets of paper
❄ A pencil or pen
❄ Scissors
❄ 3 large pieces of orange fabric or felt (each one needs to be bigger than the size you want your stocking to be)
❄ 1 piece of white felt
❄ Pins
❄ Fabric scissors
❄ Fabric glue or a needle and thread to sew the stocking together
❄ Black and red fabric or permanent markers
❄ Cotton wool
❄ Googly eyes
❄ A piece of red felt for the scarf

Follow the steps to make a Christmas stocking as *fantastic* as **Mr Fox** himself!

What to do

1

Draw identical stocking shapes on two of your pieces of paper, then **cut out** the shapes.

2

Lay the paper stocking shapes on the pieces of orange fabric or felt and use **pins** to hold them in place. Use fabric scissors to carefully **cut round** each of the stocking shapes.

3

Lay the two stocking shapes one **on top** of the other, then pin them together, leaving room to sew around the edges. Carefully **sew** the edges together, leaving the top of the stocking open.

If you would prefer not to sew, use fabric glue to stick the inside edges of the two stockings together, leaving an opening at the top and plenty of room inside for your presents.

4

Using the remaining orange felt, **cut out** a tail shape, two paws and two small triangles for the ears. Using the white felt, cut out a **tummy** and a white strip for the bottom of your fox's **face**.

5

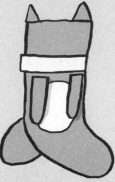

Glue or sew the cut-outs on to your stocking. Add the fox's ears, tail and tummy, then his paws and white face.

6

Use white **cotton wool** to make the ears and tail fluffy, as shown, and stick on the **googly eyes**. Using your fabric markers, **draw** on a little red mouth and black nose (or stick on red and black felt).

7

Cut out two strips of **red felt** to make the **scarf** and cut a little fringe at the end of the piece that will be dangling down.

8

Make a little **loop** out of a piece of orange felt and sew it to the top of your stocking, so that you can **hang it up** on Christmas Eve!

Ask a grown-up to help you with this craft!

Find the Gifts

Help Mr and Mrs Fox find **four** fantastic Christmas gifts for their young foxes in the grid

C	H	I	C	K	E	N	E	N	B
V	O	B	A	P	C	E	A	C	T
D	E	N	R	B	F	I	G	E	U
I	C	H	I	J	A	Q	O	A	R
A	G	E	A	S	K	B	C	F	K
H	C	P	T	U	D	N	K	H	E
B	P	Y	J	A	M	A	S	E	Y
C	N	B	E	I	A	G	H	J	D
F	A	S	A	D	T	B	A	C	A
P	N	E	C	K	S	C	A	R	F

Answers: CHICKEN, TURKEY, PYJAMAS, NECK SCARF

UN HAPPY
Christmas to You!

Roald Dahl **hated** family-picture Christmas cards! Make an 'Unhappy Christmas!' card for Boggis, Bunce and Bean from Mr Fox and his family. On the front draw a very **happy** picture of the foxes dining on all the farmers' food – it'll make them **wild** with rage!

Seasonal
Winter Warmer

You will need

* ❄ A peeler
* ❄ A food processor
* ❄ A fine-mesh sieve
* ❄ A small saucepan
* ❄ A mug
* ❄ Strong arms
* ❄ 4 apples – a sweet variety
* ❄ 1 lime, squeezed
* ❄ 2 tablespoons of sugar
* ❄ 1 cinnamon stick, broken into 3 pieces
* ❄ 1 carton of apple juice

Ask a grown-up to help you with the food processor and the cooking!

What to do

1   **Peel** and **core** the apples.

2   Place in the **food processor** with the lime juice and **puree** for 4 minutes.

3   **Push** through a very fine **sieve** into a small saucepan.

4   Add the **sugar** and the broken **cinnamon** stick.

5   Heat gently while **stirring**.

6   Push through a sieve again and then add the **apple juice**.

7   Pour into a mug and it's **ready**.

Mrs Fox's Christmas **Feast**

Help Mrs Fox make the most **sumptuous** Christmas feast! Write the menu and then **draw** the delicious meal in the middle of the table.

✳ ✳ ✳ Menu ✳ ✳ ✳

On the

SEVENTH

day of
Christmas

**my true love
gave to me . . .**

SEVEN
GIGANTUOUS
INSECTS

GIANT
Peach Bauble

Follow the steps to make your own giant peach **bauble**. It'll be too big for your Christmas tree of course, but nearly big enough to **flatten** James's horrible aunts!

You will need

❄ An old football
❄ Peach-coloured chalk paint
❄ A paintbrush
❄ Orange or gold glitter glue
❄ Giant green ribbon
❄ Strong glue (and a grown-up to help you with it!)

1

Paint your football **peach** with the chalk paint.

Ask a grown-up to help you with this!

2

Once the **paint** is dry, **decorate** the ball with **glitter glue**.

3

When the glitter is **dry**, ask a **grown-up** to help you attach your **green ribbon** to the top of the ball using strong glue.

4

Put your **giant peach bauble** next to your Christmas tree – it'll be far too **enormous** to hang on the branches, but it might come in handy should you have any **annoying relatives** in your house over the Christmas holidays!

Fruity Christmas Tree

Make a fruitful festive feast big enough for James and his giant insect friends with this lovely fruity Christmas tree! It makes the perfect centrepiece and tastes **delicious** too!

You will need

* 1 large ripe pineapple
* A sharp knife
* A star-shaped cookie cutter
* A packet of cocktail sticks or small skewers
* 1 ripe pear
* A selection of other fruit to decorate your tree, e.g. apples, bananas, satsumas and tinned peaches.

Note
The fruit types above are just **suggestions**. You can use a mixture of your favourite fruits to **decorate** your tree.

What to do

1 Ask a **grown-up** to help you cut the top and bottom off your **pineapple** and remove all the **skin**. Cut a 4cm-thick slice off one end.

2 Use your **star-shaped** cookie cutter to make this slice into a **pineapple star** for the top of your tree.

3 **Peel** your pear and cut off the **bottom** and **top**, then use a cocktail stick to attach it to the remaining pineapple to make a **tree shape**.

4 Use another **cocktail stick** to attach the pineapple star **on top** of the pear.

5 Add the selection of **different-coloured** fruit to decorate your tree, using the cocktail sticks to attach them. For the **larger** fruit, you can use the **cookie cutter** to make star-shaped pieces.

Eat and enjoy!

Ask a grown-up to help you with the cutting!

Giant Peach Piñata

Continue the fruit theme by making this **giant** peach piñata, which is full of dried fruit. It's perfect for **entertaining** everyone at any Christmas bash!

You will need
- ❄ A large bowl
- ❄ 130g flour
- ❄ 375ml water
- ❄ A spoon or whisk
- ❄ A large balloon
- ❄ Newspaper
- ❄ Scissors
- ❄ Peach-coloured tissue paper
- ❄ Glue
- ❄ A sharp pencil
- ❄ Green ribbon or string to hang up your piñata
- ❄ Green card
- ❄ Dried fruit in little bags for the contents

1 First, make a papier-mâché **peach**. Mix together your flour and water in a large bowl to make a thin **paste**.

2 **Blow up** your balloon and **tie the end** to secure it.

3 Tear or **cut up** your newspaper into strips, then **dip** them into the paste and lay them over your balloon, leaving a **hole** (big enough for your bags of dried fruit).

4 Keep **layering** on the strips until your balloon is covered with about **four layers** of newspaper. Leave the balloon to **dry** for at least 24 hours.

5 Cut your tissue paper into **long strips**. Then cut into the strips to make **fringes**, as shown.

6 **Glue** the tissue paper on to your piñata. Cover the whole thing, **except** for the opening at the top.

7 Ask a **grown-up** to help you **pop** the balloon with a **sharp pencil** or scissors.

8 Ask a **grown-up** to help you use a pencil or scissors to make **two small holes** at the top of your piñata. Then **thread** your ribbon or string through the holes and make a **loop**.

9 **Fill** your piñata with your bags of **dried fruit**.

10 Cut out two **leaf shapes** and a **stem** from your **green card** and glue them at the top of your piñata to **hide** the hole.

11 Hang up your **giant peach piñata**, then get everyone ready to bash it!

On the

EIGHTH

day of
Christmas

**my true love
gave to me . . .**

EIGHT

CRAFTY

CROCODILES

(one of them is **enormous**)

SECRET
Christmas Plans *and*
CLEVER
Christmas Tricks

Help the **Enormous** Crocodile come up with a special Christmas-themed list of **secret plans** and clever tricks! Remember he's a greedy, grumptious **BRUTE** who loves to guzzle up little girls and boys!

My secret Christmas plans and clever Christmas tricks

For example:
Wrap up an empty box as a present!

Christmas
Camouflage

Draw some special Christmas **disguises** to help the Enormous Crocodile blend into his **festive** surroundings, ready to jump out and SURPRISE children!

Christmas Snappers!

Make these Enormous Crocodile **Christmas crackers and get snapping!**

You will need

❄ A large piece of white paper
❄ Pens or pencils to draw your design
❄ Googly eyes
❄ Glue
❄ Kitchen-roll tubes (one tube makes two crackers)
❄ Scissors
❄ Cracker snaps
❄ Jokes to put inside (you could use the Twits' jokes from page 30)
❄ Little gifts or chocolates that will fit inside your kitchen-roll tube
❄ Sticky tape
❄ Green ribbon or string

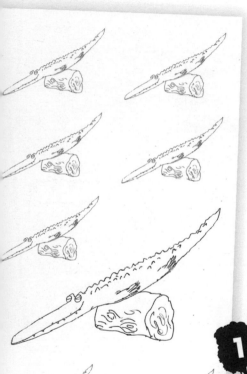

What to do

1

Draw and colour a repeating pattern of Enormous Crocodiles on your white paper, then glue on **googly eyes**. Make sure the crocodiles are quite small, like this.

2

Cut your kitchen-roll tube in **half**, then lay a cracker snap inside it and put it on the **back** of your Enormous Crocodile paper, as shown.

3

Cut enough paper to **wrap round** your tube and cracker snap.

4

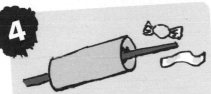

Put your **joke** and **gift** inside the kitchen-roll tube.

5

Carefully **wrap** the paper round the tube and **tape it** in place, making sure the gift and joke stay inside.

6

Pinch each end of the paper tightly and **tie** with your green ribbon or string. Make sure that they are tied nice and **tight** so that nothing can **fall out** of your tube.

7

Make some more Enormous Crocodile crackers and **get snapping!**

Roald Dahl's Christmas Gift Switch

Someone's been up to **mischief** and jumbled up all the Christmas presents! **Draw lines** to match the gifts to the **right** characters.

Answers: Enormous Crocodile – monkey; Mr Fox – chicken; the BFG – snozzcumber; Mr Wonka – chocolate; Matilda – books

99

On the

NINTH

day of
Christmas

my true love
gave to me . . .

NINE
SPOONFULS OF
MEDICINE

George's Merry Medicine

What do **you** think would be in George's special **Christmas** medicine? List the ingredients here.

Mince Pies

What Happens Next?

Draw what you think would happen to someone if they were to try George's special **CHRISTMAS** medicine.

Grandma Kranky's Guide to a Kranky Christmas

Fancy a **CRANKY** Christmas this year? Learn from the best with **George's grandma's guide** to having the crankiest Christmas!

1
Doze through as **much** of Christmas as you can. It's a **miserable** time of year and not worth being awake for.

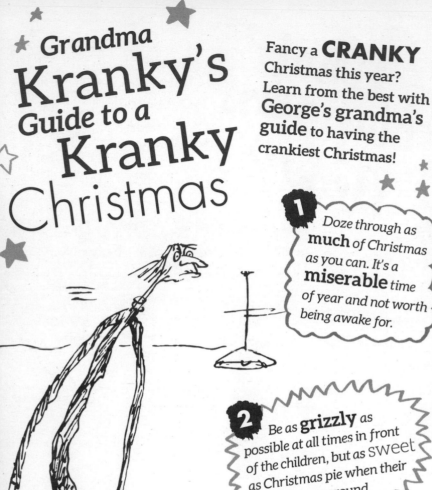

2
Be as **grizzly** as possible at all times in front of the children, but as sweet as Christmas pie when their parents are around.

3
NEVER SMILE.
Even if you actually get a Christmas present **you like** for once. (**Extremely** unlikely.)

4

DO NOT under any circumstances buy **anyone** other than yourself a **Christmas present**.

5

Insist that **all** children make you a nice cup of tea as often as possible, even if they are trying to open their **silly** Christmas presents. And be sure to tell them **exactly** how to make it – they always get it wrong, the little **brats! NEVER** settle for the first cup you are given.

6

SCARE all children with nasty, **gruesome** Christmas tales and make them run and **hide!** That'll teach them to ask you to read them bedtime stories! Fingers crossed you'll **never** be asked again and can continue your evening **doze** in peace.

7

If you accidentally make eye contact with a child, **complain**, **grumble** or **gripe** instantly. They'll soon move on.

8

Do not under **any** circumstances wish any child a 'Merry Christmas'. Christmas is **not** merry, it's just another miserable day of the year.

Have a Kranky Christmas, you little maggots!

Crystal Candy Canes

George was **amazed** at what his homemade medicine could do! Try this salt-crystal experiment and be amazed by your very own homemade crystallized candy canes!

You will need

* One red and one white pipe cleaner, plus one more of any colour, for each crystal candy cane you want to make
* Glass jars (one for each candy cane)
* Water
* A saucepan
* A cooker (and **a grown-up** to help you boil water)
* Salt
* Clothes pegs
* Ribbon to hang your candy canes on your Christmas tree
* Scissors

What to do

1

Twist one **red** and one **white** pipe cleaner together to make each candy cane.

2

Fill the jars you need almost to the top with water, then pour the water into a saucepan and **ask a grown-up** to help heat it for you.

3

Heat the water until it boils, then add **salt** to it until the salt starts to **crystallize** on the surface of the water.

4

ASK A GROWN-UP

to turn off the cooker and, over the sink, carefully pour the water into the jars.

5

Tie an **extra** pipe cleaner to the bottom of each of your candy canes, then **clip** a clothes peg to it, as shown, and **suspend** your candy canes in the jars of salt water.

6

Put your jars in a **sunny spot** and your candy canes should begin to **crystallize** in a few hours. It's best to leave them for about **three days**, if possible. Then, carefully remove your candy canes and admire the amazing crystals that have formed!

7

Carefully tie some **ribbon** to your candy canes and hang them on your tree to **sparkle** in the fairy lights!

Christmas
Alliteration

'**Marvellous Medicine**' is a great example of *alliteration* – where two words start with the **same** letter or sound, and are close to each other. How many *different* examples of Christmas alliteration can you think of? **List them** on this page. We have added a few to start you off.

terrible **t**urkey

Christmas **c**rackers

pretty **p**resents

Alternative

Christmas Messages

It gets a bit boring writing the same Christmas message in every card and on every gift tag. Think of some fun ones and write them down here. You could even use some of your alliteration examples from the opposite page.

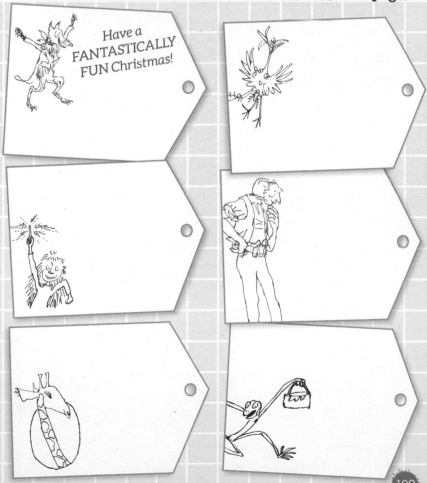

Have a FANTASTICALLY FUN Christmas!

On the

TENTH

day of
Christmas

my true love
gave to me . . .

TEN
CHOMPING
TORTOISES

Festive Tortoises

Give these tortoises a **festive** makeover! How about a knitted Christmas-tree hat **or a scarf** with twinkling lights? Or you could even try **gift-wrapping** one of them with a bright red Christmas **bow**, ready to send to Mrs Silver!

A Tortoise's
Twistmas Dinner

Design the **perfect** Christmas menu for all Mr Hoppy's tortoises. Remember, **every dish must include cabbage!**

Today's Christmas Menu
Starters

. . . .

. . . .

. . . .

Mains

. . . .

. . . .

. . . .

Desserts

. . . .

. . . .

. . . .

CHOMP, CHOMP!

Draw a **picture** of ten chomping tortoises **chomping** down their **Christmas dinner**.

Top **10** Christmas Firsts

1 The first **Christmas card** was sent in the UK in **1843**.

2 The first **charity Christmas card** was sent in **1949** – all profits went to UNICEF (the United Nations Children's Fund).

3 In 1957, Queen Elizabeth II delivered the first televised royal **Christmas message** live from the Long Library at her residence in Sandringham, Norfolk. It was the twenty-fifth anniversary of her grandfather George V's first Christmas message via wireless radio.

4 The first **Christmas cracker** was pulled in **1846**.

5 The first **advent calendar** was made in Germany in **1851** ...

6 ... but the first **chocolate-filled advent calendar** wasn't produced until a whole century later.

7 In **1848**, Prince Albert – Queen Victoria's husband – introduced the first **Christmas tree** to Windsor Castle. Soon, the rest of the UK joined in.

8 The first **Christmas fairy lights** appeared just three years after Thomas Edison invented the light bulb. One of the American inventor's friends – Edward Johnson – used them to decorate his tree in **1882**.

9 **Tinsel** was invented in Germany in **1610**. The first garland was made of real silver.

10 The first **English collection of carols** was published in **1521**, but they were probably sung much earlier than that.

On the

ELEVENTH

day of
Christmas

**my true love
gave to me . . .**

ELEVEN

FOULSOME

WITCHES

Christmas with the Witches

1 **Children.** Children love Christmas, and Christmas is all about children. And there's nothing witches despise more than wretched children!

2 **People busy shopping.** Everywhere is so busy with silly people buying stupid presents for their ridiculous families, so it's much harder to 'vurk'. How can a witch be expected to sneak up on bratty children, squish them, squiggle them, and make them disappear in all the chaos?

3 **Christmas trees.** People's houses are smelly with all those stinky children in them, but when they have Christmas trees as well, they're an abomination to the senses, especially to those with larger-than-average nose-holes, like witches!

4 **Woolly hats.** Wearing a wig makes the scalp itchy enough, without having to wear a hat to keep warm as well!

5 Pretending to be happy it's Christmas. It's hard pretending to be a pathetic human all the time without having to be a happy human just because it's Christmastime, again!

6 Clean children. For some reason children seem to get washed even more at Christmastime, so they stink of the freshest dogs' droppings imaginable. It's putrid.

7 Socks. Every year, no matter what, someone always buys socks as a Christmas present. And what use are socks to a witch with no toes?

8 Hotels getting booked up. It's difficult for The Grand High Witch to host all her annual meetings at this busy time of year.

9 People being nice. There's nothing more annoying than seeing humans being nice to each other. Especially when they're nice to those filthy little children.

10 Children visiting Santa. *Eurgh!* The queues of stinking children waiting for Santa are just too much to bear. The smell is so concentrated, it's enough to make a witch vomit on the spot.

11 Writing Christmas cards. Even with blue spit ready to use as ink, it seems like such a waste of time writing Christmas cards, just to pretend that a witch cares that everyone has a 'Merry Christmas!' *What rot!*

Witches' Gloves

Wreath

Follow the instructions to make a Christmas wreath made of witches' gloves!

You will need
* ❄ Card or a large paper plate
* ❄ Scissors
* ❄ Lots of thin green card and thin red card
* ❄ A pencil
* ❄ Glue
* ❄ Red ribbon or string for hanging the wreath

What to do

1

Cut out a cardboard ring from a sheet of card or a large paper plate.

2

Draw round your hand on the green card **at least** sixteen times so that the 'gloves' will stretch all the way round your cardboard ring.

3

Carefully **cut out** the gloves and glue them on to the card ring, allowing the wrists to **overlap**, as shown.

4

Cut out some **red berries** from the red card and glue them on to make the gloves look a little like holly.

5

Your witches' gloves wreath is ready to **hang up**! Tie some ribbon or string to the top of your wreath and ask a **grown-up** to help you hang it up.

The Witches' Wicked Christmas Fortune Teller

Give your friends and family a **shock** by telling them a wicked fortune this Christmas!

Witches' Wicked Fortune Ideas

On Christmas Day you'll be fed Formula 86 and turn into a mouse! • **All you'll get for Christmas is an itchy wig!** • **A witch is going to kick you up, up and away!** • *You're going to wake up on Christmas morning as bald as a boiled egg!* • **Your stocking will be as empty as a witch's heart!** • *Your face will be eaten away by maggots on Christmas Day!* • **You'll be squished by a witch this Christmas!** • *If you grow a tail, it'll be chopped off immediately!*

What to do

1 Fold your square of paper in half, bringing the **bottom left** corner up to the **top right** corner, then unfold it.

2 Fold your paper in half the other way, then unfold it. You should now have four triangular shapes on your piece of paper.

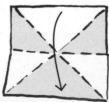

3 Fold your paper in half again by folding the top edge to the bottom edge, then unfold it.

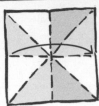

4 Fold your paper in half by folding the left edge to the right edge, as shown, then unfold it.

5 Fold all four corners into the centre, as shown.

6 Turn your paper over and then fold all four corners into the centre again, as shown.

7 Label the triangles with different numbers 1–8.

8 Write a wicked fortune underneath each label and close the flaps. See opposite for wicked fortune ideas.

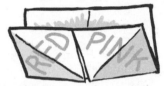

9 Fold the bottom half of the paper to the top. Label each of the four outside flaps a different colour. Tuck your thumbs and fingers into the openings under the triangles. Now you can play!

HOW TO PLAY: Have a friend pick a colour. Spell out the colour as you open the fortune teller lengthways and then widthwise (e.g. if they pick 'red', move the fortune teller three times: R-E-D). Ask your friend to pick a number from those visible inside, then move the fortune teller that many times. Ask your friend to pick another number. Open the flap they picked and read them their wicked Christmas fortune!

On the
TWELFTH
day of
Christmas

**my true love
gave to me . . .**

TWELVE
TWISTMAS
TALES

TWISTED Christmas Tales

Roald Dahl is **famous** for coming up with **fantastic twists** on traditional rhymes and fairy tales. Read some of his rhymes on pages 130–153, then use these pages to come up with **your own twisted** Christmas tales! Write or draw your ideas here. Why not add an **exploding** Christmas pudding to The Emperor's New Clothes, or a **flying** reindeer to Dick Whittington and His Cat and see what happens? Let your festive **imagination** run wild!

The Emperor's New Clothes

The Royal Tailor, Mister Ho,
Had premises on Savile Row,
And thence the King would make his way
At least a dozen times a day.
His passion was for gorgeous suits
And sumptuous cloaks and fur-lined boots
And brilliant waistcoats lined in red,
Hand-sewn with gold and silver thread.
Within the Palace things were grand,
With valets everywhere on hand
To hang the clothes and clean and press
And help the crazy King to dress.
But clothes are very dangerous things,
Especially for wealthy kings.
This King had gone to pot so fast,
His clothes came first, his people last.

One valet who was seen to leave
A spot of gravy on a sleeve
Was hung from rafters by his hair
And left forever dangling there.
Another who had failed to note
A fleck of dust upon a coat
Was ordered to be boiled alive,
A fate not easy to survive.
And one who left a pinch of snuff
Upon a pale-blue velvet cuff
Was minced inside a large machine
And reappeared as margarine.

Oh, what a beastly horrid King!
The people longed to do him in!
And so a dozen brainy men
Met secretly inside a den
To formulate a subtle plot
To polish off this royal clot.
Up spake the very brainiest man
Who cried, 'I've got a wizard plan.
Please come with me. We all must go
To see the royal tailor, Ho.
We'll tell him very strong and true
Exactly what he's got to do.'
So thus the secret plans were laid
And all arrangements quickly made.

T'was winter-time with lots of snow
And every day the King would go
To ski a bit before he dined
In ski-suits specially designed.
But even on these trips he'd stop
To go into the tailor's shop.
'O Majesty!' cried Mister Ho.
'I cannot wait to let you know
That I've contrived at last to get
From secret weavers in Tibet
A cloth so magical and fine,
So unbelievably divine,
You've never seen its like before
And never will do any more!'
The King yelled out, 'I'll buy the lot!
I'll purchase every yard you've got!'
The tailor smiled and bowed his head.
'O honoured sire,' he softly said,
'This marvellous magic cloth has got
Amazing ways to keep you hot,
And even when it's icy cold
You still feel warm as molten gold.
However hard the north wind blows
You still won't need your underclothes.'

The King said, 'If it's all that warm,
I'll have a ski-ing uniform!
I want ski-trousers and a jacket!
I don't care if it costs a packet!
Produce the cloth. I want to see
This marvellous stuff you're selling me.'
The tailor, feigning great surprise,
Said, 'Sire, it's here before your eyes.'
The King said, 'Where? Just tell me where.'
'It's in my hands, O King, right here!'
The King yelled, tearing at his hair,
'Don't be an ass! There's nothing there!'
The tailor cried, 'Hold on, I pray!
There's something I forgot to say!
This cloth's invisible to fools
And nincompoops and other ghouls.
For brainless men who're round the twist
This cloth does simply not exist!
But seeing how you're wise and bright,
I'm sure it glistens in your sight.'

Now right on cue, exactly then,
In burst the dozen brainy men.
They shouted, 'Oh, what lovely stuff!
We want some too! D'you have enough?'
Extremely calm, the tailor stands,
With nothing in his empty hands,
And says, 'No, no! this gorgeous thing
Is only for my lord, the King.'
The King, not wanting to admit
To being a proper royal twit,
Cried out, 'Oh, isn't it divine!
I want it all! It's mine! It's mine!
I want a ski-ing outfit most
So I can keep as warm as toast!'
The brainy men all cried, 'Egad!
Oh, Majesty, you lucky lad!
You'll feel so cosy in the snow
With temps at zero and below!'
Next day the tailor came to fit
The costume on the royal twit.
The brainy men all went along
To see that nothing should go wrong.

The tailor said, 'Strip naked, sire.
This suit's so warm you won't require
Your underclothes or pants or vest
Or even hair upon your chest.'
And now the clever Mister Ho
Put on the most terrific show
Of dressing up the naked King
In nothing – not a single thing.

'That's right, sir, slip your arm in there,
And now I'll zip you up right here.
Do you feel comfy? Does it fit?
Or should I take this in a bit?'
Now during this absurd charade,
And while the King was off his guard,
The brainy men, so shrewd and sly,
Had turned the central heating high.
The King, although completely bare,
With not a stitch of underwear,
Began to sweat and mop his brow,
And cried, 'I do believe you now!
I feel as though I'm going to roast!
This suit will keep me warm as toast!'

The Queen, just then, came strolling through
With ladies of her retinue.
They stopped. They gasped. There stood the King
As naked as a piece of string,
As naked as a popinjay,
With not a fig-leaf in the way.
He shouted, striking up a pose,
'Behold my marvellous ski-ing clothes!
These clothes will keep me toasty-warm
In hail or sleet or snow or storm!'

Some ladies blushed and hid their eyes
And uttered little plaintive cries.
But some, it seemed, enjoyed the pleasures
Of looking at the royal treasures.
A brazen wench cried, 'Oh my hat!
Hey girls, just take a look at that!'
The Queen, who'd seen it all before,
Made swiftly for the nearest door.
The King cried, 'Now I'm off to ski!
You ladies want to come with me?'
They shook their heads, so off he went,
A madman off on pleasure bent.
The crazy King put on his skis,
And now, oblivious to the freeze,
He shot outdoors and ski'd away,
Still naked as a popinjay.
And thus this fool, so lewd and squalid,
In half an hour was frozen solid.
And all the nation cried, 'Heigh-ho!
The King's deep-frozen in the snow!'

Dick Whittington and His Cat

Dick Whittington had oft been told
That London's streets were paved with gold.
'We'd better have a look at that,'
He murmured to his faithful cat.
And finally they made it there
And finished up in Berkeley Square.
So far so good, but Dicky knew
That he must find some work to do.
Imagine, if you can, his joy
At being made the pantry-boy
To Lord and Lady Hellespont!
What more could any young lad want?

His Lordship's house was huge and warm,
Each footman wore a uniform,
Rich carpets lay on all the floors,
And big brass door-knobs on the doors.
Why, Whittington had never seen
A house so marvellously clean,
Although, regrettably, his cat
Soon did some things to alter that.
His Lordship kicked the cat so hard
It landed in a neighbour's yard,
But still each morning on the floor
It did what it had done before.

His Lordship shouted, 'Fetch my gun!
I'll nail the blighter on the run!
Call up the beaters! Flush him out!
I know he's somewhere hereabout!'
It is a fact that wealthy men
Do love to shoot things now and then.
They shoot at partridge, pheasant, grouse,
Though not so much *inside* the house.
But now His Lordship stalks the brute
With gun in hand, prepared to shoot.
He crouches down behind a chair.

Ah-ha! What's moving over there?
Of course the poor sap couldn't know
His wife was on the portico,
Locked in a passionate embrace
With second footman, Albert Grace.
The gun goes off, *bang-bang,*
    boom-boom!
The noise explodes around the room.
You should have seen the lady jump
As grapeshot struck her in
    the rump,

And in the kitchen, washing up,
Dick jumps and breaks a precious cup.
This is a crime no decent cook
Could bring herself to overlook.
This cook, a brawny powerful wench,
Put Whittington across the bench
And systematically began
To beat him with a frying-pan
Which she had very quickly got
From off the stove, all sizzling hot.
Poor Whittington, his rump aflame,
At last escapes the fearsome dame
And runs outside across the street,
Clutching his steaming smoking seat.

The cat, now very frightened, said,
'Let's beat it quick before we're dead.'
At that point, with an angry shout
Her Ladyship comes flying out.
(Although indeed she had been shot,
It wasn't in a vital spot.)
She yells, 'I'm on the run as well!
Old Hellespont can go to hell!'
Just then, a peal of bells rings out.
Each bell begins to sing and shout,
And Dick could quite distinctly hear
A message coming through the air.
He actually could hear his name!
He heard the Bells of Bow proclaim –

> *Turn again, Whittington,*
> *Thou worthy citizen,*
> *Turn again, Whittington,*
> *Lord Mayor of London!*

'Lord Mayor of London!' cries the cat.
'I've never heard such rot as that!'
Her Ladyship butts in and yells,
'The cat is right! That's not the *bells*!
Bow church has got a crazy vicar,
A famous and fantastic tricker,
A disco king, a hi-fi buff,
A whizz on electronic stuff.
He's rigged up speakers in the steeple
To fool dim-witted country people.
Listen, you poor misguided youth,
In London no one tells the truth!'

She looks at Dick. Dick looks at her.
She smiles and says, 'My dear sir,
I must say I prefer your face
To second footman, Albert Grace.
I think we'd make a nifty team,
With me the strawberries, you the cream.'
The cat cries, 'Dick, you do not want
To fool with Lady Hellespont!
These females from the upper-classes
Spend their lives in making passes!'
At this point, with a mighty roar,
Lord Hellespont bursts through the door.
He sees his wife. He lifts his gun.
The lady screams and starts to run.

Once more, with a colossal thump,
The grapeshot strikes her in the rump.
'Oh gosh!' Dick cries. 'I do declare
That no one's bum seems safe in here!'
The furious red-faced lady stands
Clutching her bottom in her hands,
And shouts, 'You quite deliberately
Pointed that filthy gun at me!'
He cries, 'I aimed it at the cat.'
The lady shouts, 'The cat my hat!
You don't think I'm believing that!'

'Oh yes, you must!' His Lordship cries,
Blinking his crafty boozy eyes.
'I simply cannot be to blame
Because *all cats* look much the same.'
The cat cried, 'That's a vicious slur!
How dare you say I look like *her*!'
Now Whittington pulls out his sword
And runs it through the noble Lord,
Shouting, 'Gadzooks! Hooray! There passes
One member of the upper-classes!'
Her Ladyship leaps high with joy
And cries, 'Well done, my scrumptious boy!
The old goat's clobbered once for all!
Now you and I can have a ball!'

The cat shouts, 'Dick, do not succumb
To blandishments from that old crumb!
And by the way, the man who told
That London's streets were paved with gold
Was telling dreadful porky-pies.'
(That's cockney rhyming-slang for lies.)
The cat went on, 'To me it seems
These streets are paved with rotten dreams.
Come home, my boy, without more fuss.
This lousy town's no place for us.'
Dick says, 'You're right,' then sighs and mumbles,
'Well well, that's how the cookie crumbles.'

New Year's
resolutions

Can you **guess** which of Roald Dahl's characters might have made these New Year's **resolutions**?

1 Repair the chocolate factory roof.

2 **Read Encyclopaedia Britannica. All of it.**

3 *Win first prize in a giant fruit and vegetable competition.*

4 NOT EAT CABBAGE SOUP – NOT THIS YEAR, NOT NEXT YEAR, NOT EVER AGAIN.

5 Inspect spaghetti suppers very thoroughly before a single strand passes my lips.

Wishing you a very **Merry Christmas** and a Happy New Year from the world of **Roald Dahl!**

Answers: 1) Charlie, 2) Matilda, 3) James, 4) The Bucket family, 5) Mr Twit.

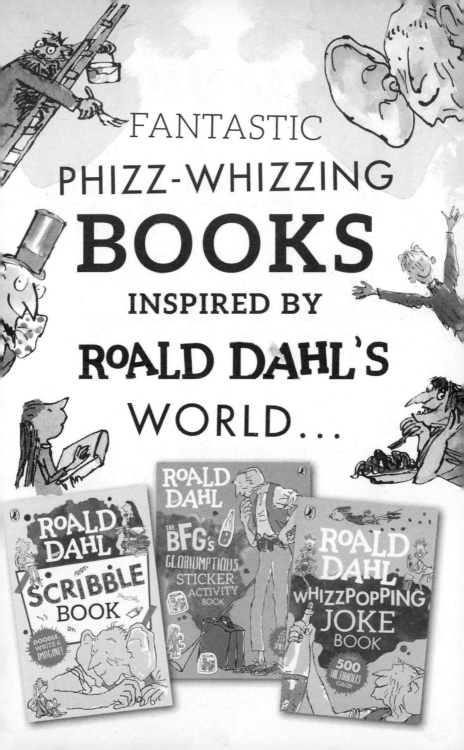

FANTASTIC
PHIZZ-WHIZZING
BOOKS
INSPIRED BY
ROALD DAHL'S
WORLD...

How Many Have You Read?

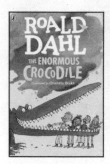

Fewer than 5?

WHOOPSY-SPLUNKERS!

You've got some reading to do!

BETWEEN 5 AND 10?
Wonderful surprises await!
Keep reading . . .

MORE THAN 10?
Whoopee!
Which was your favourite?

Have **YOU** PLAYED the **FANTASTICALLY** FUN **ROALD DAHL** apps?

ROALD DAHL DAY

CELEBRATE

THE **PHIZZ-WHIZZING**

WORLD of **ROALD DAHL**

EVERY YEAR on

13th SEPTEMBER!

JOIN THE PARTY AT
www.roalddahl.com